Sign Language for Kids
Activity Book

SIGN LANGUAGE FOR KIDS ACTIVITY BOOK

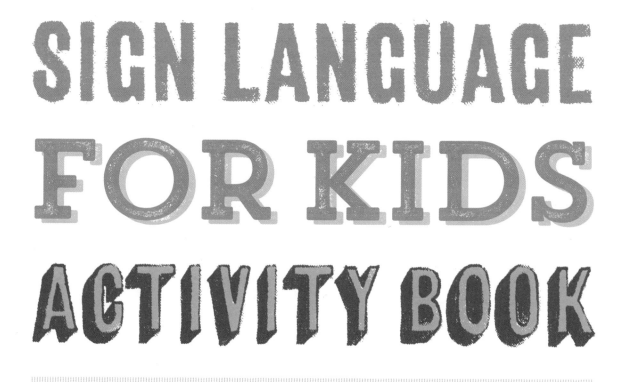

50 Fun Games and Activities to Start Signing

TARA ADAMS

ILLUSTRATIONS BY NATALIA SANABRIA

callisto publishing
an imprint of Sourcebooks

For my smallest students,
whose tiny hands remind me what a gift
it is to connect and communicate—
no matter the language.

CONTENTS

INTRODUCTION

WELCOME TO the *Sign Language for Kids Activity Book!* This book will help you start learning how to communicate in a whole new way using your hands. If you already know some American Sign Language (ASL), the games and activities inside will help you improve your signing in fun, unique ways.

This book has two parts:

The first section of this book presents illustrations and descriptions for more than 180 signs, plus the signed alphabet and numbers 1-100. I carefully picked some of the most important ones to know. They will help you begin communicating in ASL as quickly as possible.

The second part of the book contains 50 activities that include both on- and off-page practice exercises, games, and puzzles. These activities are designed to improve your memory of the signs you learned and will help you build fluency so that you feel comfortable and confident communicating with sign language.

WHAT IS ASL?

ASL is a visual language that is expressed through our hands, facial expressions, and body language. The greatest thing about visual languages is that they are not dependent on sound or speech, so they are especially useful for those who have difficulty hearing and/or speaking.

ASL uses specific signs for words and concepts, as well as rule-based body language and movements to communicate grammar and syntax. Since ASL is a visual language, we are also able to use the space around our bodies, facial expression, and directionality. Due to its visual nature, many words we use to build sentences in English are not necessary in ASL, such as *it, is, am, be, are,* and *to.* This means we are able to get our point across with fewer signs.

In ASL, each sign represents a specific word or concept. Sometimes a sign has an exact English word that it represents. Sometimes an English word has multiple meanings and therefore will have multiple signs, such as **RUN** for president or **RUN** out of milk.

Occasionally, there is more than one sign for a word due to sign variations in different regions of the country. This is especially true for food and animal signs. I worked hard to select the most commonly used signs, but interacting with your local signing community will help you find out if some of the signs used in your area are different from the ones in this book. Always be respectful of the signs your local community is using.

While ASL uses English words as concepts to express ideas, the grammar of ASL is a bit different. ASL is a topic-comment based language. This means that the topic of the statement comes first and the comment follows. For example, in English we might say, "I want to play outside." In ASL, "**PLAY OUTSIDE**" would be signed first, since that is the topic, then "**I WANT**" would come last, because that is the comment.

In ASL, question words and negations tend to fall at the end of a sentence. In English we might say, "Where do you live?" In ASL, since the question word falls at the end, we would sign, "**YOU LIVE, WHERE?**" An example of expressing negation at the end of a sentence would be, "I don't want to go to sleep." In ASL, we would sign, "**SLEEP, I DON'T WANT.**"

There are also certain facial expressions to make for a yes/no question or a "WH" (who, what, when, where, why, how, which) question. A yes/no expression is made with your eyebrows arching upward and your head leaning forward. Express WH questions with your eyebrows squinted and your head tilted slightly to the side.

Facial expression is also very important for communicating feelings and intensity. The difference between the words **TIRED** and **EXHAUSTED** would be expressed with an exaggerated facial expression and sign intensity. You probably already do this without realizing it when speaking English. Think about what your face looks like when you are excited about something, or how it looks when you are angry. When signing, you'd use these same expressions to help you get your point across.

HOW TO READ THE SIGNS IN THIS BOOK

As you use the sign illustrations in this book, keep in mind that all signs are drawn from the signer's perspective. All of the models are right-handed, so if you are right-handed you will be copying the signs in reverse. Picture yourself in the same position as the model as you practice the signs. If you are left-handed, then you will follow the signs as if you are looking at yourself in the mirror. In signs with hands outlined in black and in red, the black hand notes where you start the sign movement, and the red hand shows where you end the movement. The arrows show the direction of the sign movement. The sign descriptions often use a letter handshape such as "B handshape" or "O handshape." This means that you will make the handshape of that letter from the manual alphabet to form the sign. If you forget a letter handshape, you can always go back to the alphabet section (page 2) to refresh your memory!

Now that you know some of the basics, we can begin learning signs. I am so honored and excited to part of your ASL journey. Are you ready to get started? Me too!

"B"   "MY NAME IS"

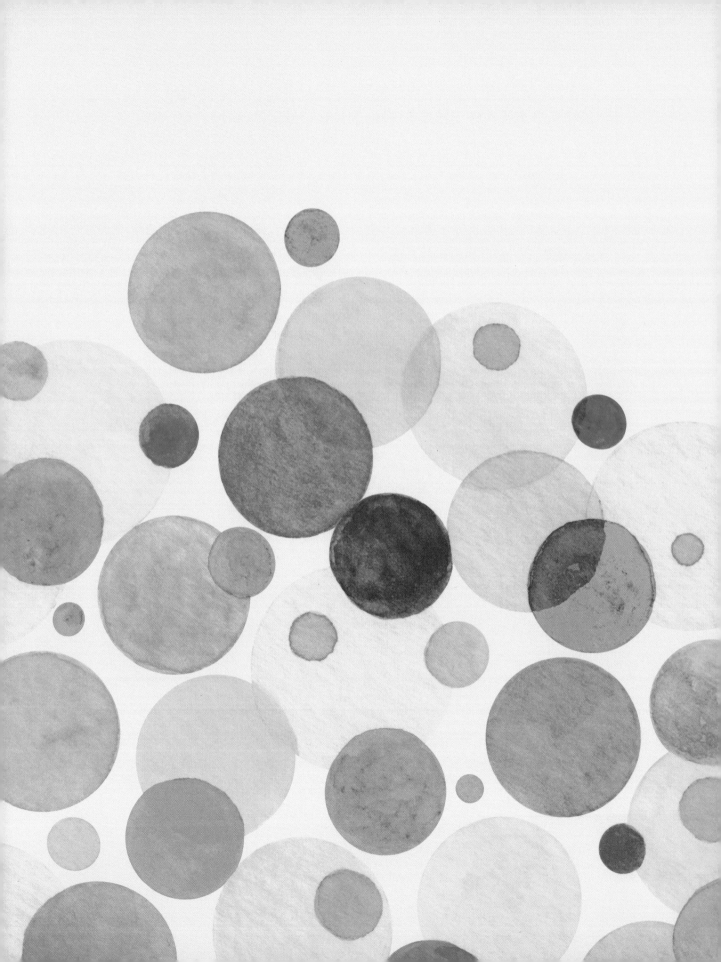

PART 1
Essential Signs

There are four letters in the alphabet that are not signed with the palm facing outward. **G** and **H** are signed with the fingers pointed to the side and the palm facing the body. **P** and **Q** are signed with both the fingers and palm down. The rest of the letters are all signed with your palm facing the person you are signing with, but with your hand a slight angle, which is more comfortable for the wrist. Take care not to strain your wrist by keeping your hand facing directly forward.

A   **B**   **C**   **D**   **E**

 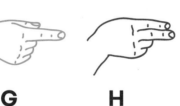  

F   **G**   **H**   **I**   **J**

K   **L**   **M**   **N**   **O**

P   **Q**   **R**   **S**   **T**

  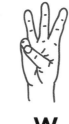 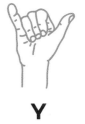

U   **V**   **W**   **X**   **Y**

Z

ASL numbers are all done with one hand. It's a very convenient way to count, as you'll soon see. Numbers 1 through 5 and 11 through 15 are signed with the palm facing your body. The rest of the numbers are signed with the palm facing away from the body. When numbers 1 through 5 are done in combination with other numbers, such as 43 or 58, they are signed with your palm forward, rather than facing your body.

1 **2** **3** **4** **5**

6 **7** **8** **9** **10**

  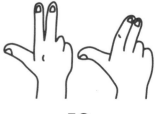

11 **12** **13**

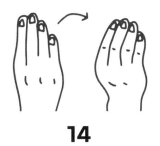 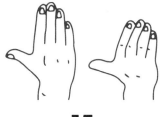

14   **15**

  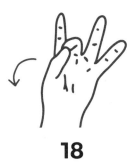

16   **17**   **18**

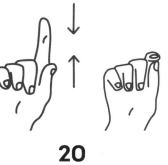

19   **20**

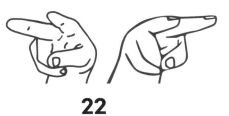

21   **22**

  **23**

 **24**

 **25**

  **26**

 **27**

28

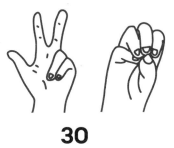 **29**

30

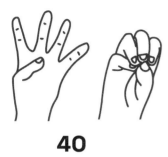 **40**

 **50**

 **60**

 **70**

 **80**

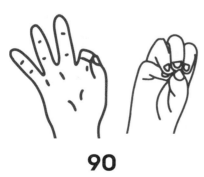 **90**

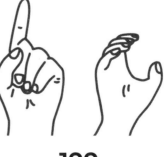 **100**

Hello

With your palm facing out, place a flat hand at the side of your forehead. Then pull your hand away from your head, as in a salute.

My name is

Put your flat hand on your chest to sign **MY**. Then, with two hands and keeping your palms facing inward, make an "H" handshape (see page 2) on both hands, then cross the top fingers over the bottom fingers and tap down two times to sign **NAME**.

What's your name?

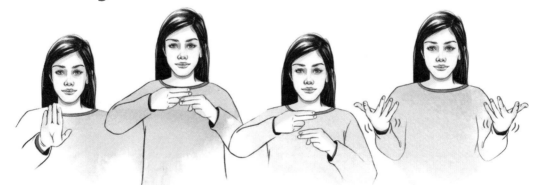

With your palm facing out, put your flat hand forward to sign **YOUR**. Then make an "H" handshape (see page 2) on each hand and tap your top fingers onto your bottom fingers two times to sign **NAME**. Last, make the sign for **WHAT** by holding out both hands open with your palms up and moving them side to side.

Nice to meet you

Start by making the sign for **NICE**: with one palm facing down and your other palm facing up, cross the hand with the palm facing down over your other palm. To sign **MEET**, with your index fingers both pointing up and palms facing each other, close your hands and bring them together until your fists touch. Last, sign **YOU** by pointing your index finger at the person you are meeting!

Please

Place a flat palm on your chest and make small circles around your heart.

Me/I

Using your index finger, point to the middle of your chest.

Sorry

This sign is similar to the sign for **PLEASE**, but you make your hand into a fist and then move it in circular motions around your heart.

Thank you/ you're welcome

With your palm facing in, make a flat handshape and touch your fingers to your mouth or chin area. Then bring your hand out toward the person to whom you are saying "thank you" or "you're welcome."

Excuse me

Hold your hands in front of you, bottom palm facing up and top palm facing down. Brush the tips of your fingers on the top hand across the tips of your fingers on your bottom hand as if you are wiping something off of your fingertips.

I love you

With your palm facing out, put up your pinkie, index finger, and thumb, and fold down the other two fingers. You can remember this one by imagining your pinkie as the "I" and your index finger and thumb making the "L" in love, and the "U" shape in the middle for "you."

Yes

With your palm facing out, make a fist and bend it down and up from the wrist. To remember this sign, think of a head nodding up and down!

No

With your palm facing out, make a "3" handshape (see page 4), keeping your fingers close together; open and close your fingers a few times. If you want to make a firm expression of "no," only open and close your fingers one time.

Maybe

Make a flat handshape with both hands, palms facing up. Then move your hands up and down alternately, as if your hands are scales weighing whether you want something or not.

Who

With your palm facing to the side, place your thumb on your chin and point your index finger. Bend your index finger repeatedly up and down.

What

Hold your hands in front of you with your palms facing up and move them side to side in opposite directions a few times, as if you are gesturing "huh?"

When

Bring the tips of your index fingers together, and then use one index finger to draw a little circle around the other fingertip, as if you're making the shape of a clock.

Where

With your palm facing out, point your index finger and wave it back and forth. This sign reminds me of a dog's tail wagging back and forth.

Why

Place your open hand next to your forehead with the palm facing in and wiggle your middle finger up and down a couple of times. You will almost be scratching your head, but not quite.

How

With both palms facing in and thumbs pointing up, and your hands in a loose fist shape, bring your knuckles together. Twist both hands forward until your palms are slightly facing up.

Which

With your palms facing inward, away from your body, make an "A" handshape (see page 2) with each hand. Then move your hands up and down alternately.

From

With both hands in the "L" handshape (see page 2), point one index finger toward the other, then bend that finger into a hook shape as you move it back toward your body.

Here

Place both hands in a flat handshape in front of you, palms facing up. Then move them both in circular motions away from each other.

Home

Close all of your fingertips together into a handshape that looks like a flat "O." Touch your fingertips to your face next your mouth and then bring them up toward your cheek.

Kitchen

Place one hand flat in front of you, palm facing up. Then put your other hand above it in a "K" handshape (see page 2). Place your "K" hand, palm-side down, on top of your upturned palm. Then flip your "K" hand over as if you are flipping a pancake.

Bedroom

Make the sign for **BED**: place your flat handshape against your cheek. To sign **ROOM**, place both hands in a flat handshape in front of you, palms facing each other. Then shift the hand positions so both palms face toward your body.

Living room

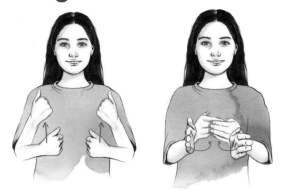

Make the sign for **LIVE** or **LIFE**: with both hands at the bottom of your chest next to your body, make two "A" handshapes (see page 2) and then move both hands up your chest toward your shoulders. To sign **ROOM**, place both hands in a flat handshape in front of you, palms facing each other. Then shift the hand positions so both palms face toward your body.

Bathroom

With your palm facing out, make a "T" handshape (see page 3) and shake the "T" handshape side to side.

TV

With your palm facing out, sign the handshapes for the letters "T" and "V" (see page 3).

Computer

Make a "C" handshape (see page 2) with one hand and bend your other arm in front of you. Make circular motions with the "C" on your other arm.

Phone

Make a "Y" handshape (see page 3) and tap it to your cheek like you are holding a phone up to your ear.

Mom

Make a "5" handshape (see page 4) and touch your thumb to the lower part of your face.

Dad

Use the same "5" handshape that you used for **MOM**, but now make it at the top of your head with your thumb touching your forehead.

Brother

Start with a closed fist touching the top of your head. Place your other hand out in front of you in a fist as well. As you bring your top hand down, stick out your index fingers on both hands and then have the top fist land on the bottom fist.

Sister

Start with a closed fist touching the bottom part of your face by your chin. Place your other hand out in front of you in a fist as well. As you bring your top hand down, stick out your index fingers on both hands and have the top fist land on the bottom fist.

Baby

Cradle your arms down in front of your stomach and rock them side to side, the way you would gently rock a baby.

Grandma

Start by making the sign for **MOM** (page 16) on the lower part of your face, then bring your open hand forward in an arching movement.

Grandpa

Start by making the sign for **DAD** (page 16) on the upper part of your face, then bring your open hand forward in an arching movement.

Aunt/uncle

For **AUNT**, make an "A" handshape (see page 2) next to the lower (female) part of the face and wiggle your fist in a slight circular or twisting motion. You can make the sign for **UNCLE** the exact same way, except with a "U" handshape next to the top (male) part of your face.

Cousin

Make a "C" handshape (see page 2) on the side of your face in the middle and wiggle your hand. To be specific about a female cousin or a male cousin, make this sign on the lower or upper part of the face, respectively.

Son/daughter

Using a flat handshape, start by referring to the male or female part of the face. For **SON**, start with your hand at your fore-head, as pictured above. For **DAUGHTER**, start with your hand near your mouth. Then bring your hand down to your other arm like you are holding a baby.

Pet

Make one hand into a fist, palm facing down. Then use your top hand to make a petting motion on your fist, like you are petting an animal. Short, quick movements sign the noun **PET**, whereas longer, more drawn-out motions sign the verb **PET**.

Cat

Make an "F" handshape (see page 2) on your cheek and pull it out to the side away from your face, like cat's whiskers.

Dog

Place one hand in front of your body and make a snapping motion with your fingers, like you are calling a dog with a snap of your fingers.

Fish

With one hand in a flat handshape and your palm facing to the side, wiggle your hand in and out like a fish swimming through the water.

Go

With your palms facing out, stick up both index fingers and move them forward at the same time, as if indicating something moving away from you.

Come

This is signed just like **GO**, with both index fingers up, but this time with your palms facing your body. Move both index fingers toward your body at the same time, as if indicating something coming closer to you.

Want

Put both hands out in front of you, palms facing up. Bend the knuckles of your fingers into a claw handshape and pull your hands toward your body, like you are pulling in something that you want.

Don't want

Instead of pulling your hands in toward you, as in the sign for **WANT**, you start with your palms facing up and then turn your palms away from your body by flipping your hands over and down, as if you are pushing away something you don't want.

Like

Start with your hand in a "5" handshape (see page 4), palm facing in, then bring your thumb and middle finger together, moving your hand away from your body as if you are pulling on a string attached to your heart.

Know

Bring all of your fingers together into a flat handshape and bend the hand slightly. Touch your fingertips to your forehead. Sometimes people tap their head a few times, or you can just tap once.

Don't like

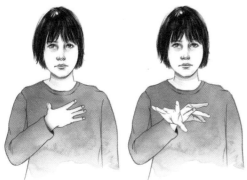

This sign is almost like the sign for **LIKE**. Start with your hand in a "5" handshape (see page 4), palm facing in, then bring your thumb and middle finger together as if you are pulling on a string attached to your heart. Instead of pulling on the string, reverse the sign away from your chest, as if you're picking something off your shirt and flicking it away.

Don't know

This one is almost like the sign for **KNOW**, but after you touch your forehead with your fingertips, twist your palm out, away from your body.

Practice

Point to the side with your non-dominant hand, palm facing toward your body. With your dominant hand, make an "A" hand-shape (see page 2) and rub it back and forth across your other index finger as if you are polishing it.

Run

With your palms facing together, make an "L" handshape (see page 2) with both hands. Wrap the index finger of one hand around the thumb of the other hand. Wiggle the index finger of the front hand as you move both of your hands forward.

Have/don't have

Make flat handshapes with both hands, palms facing in toward the body. Bend them slightly at the bottom knuckle and touch the tips of your fingers of both hands on your upper chest, just inside your shoulders. To sign **DON'T HAVE**, shake your head side to side when making this sign.

Understand/ don't understand

With your palm facing in, make a fist and hold it up to the side of your forehead, then flick your index finger upward. To remember the sign, think of a lightbulb turning on in your head. To sign that you **DON'T UNDERSTAND**, do this sign while shaking your head side to side.

Misunderstand

Make a "K" handshape (see page 2) and touch your forehead with your index finger, then rotate your hand to touch your forehead with your middle finger.

Say/tell

With your palm facing in, touch your index finger to your mouth or chin. Then move your hand away from your body, keeping your palm facing in, like a word coming out of your mouth.

Think

Touch your index finger to your forehead as if pointing to a thought that's in your head.

Talk

With your palm facing to the side, make a "4" handshape (see page 4). Tap your index finger against your mouth or chin a few times, like lots of words coming out of your mouth.

Guess/miss

Create a "C" handshape (see page 2) near the side of your face and move your hand across the front of your face and close your hand into a fist. This is also the sign for **MISS**, as in "I missed the bus" (but not the same sign for when you're missing something or someone).

Stop

Hold out one hand in a flat handshape with your palm facing up, then drop the other flat hand, palm facing to the side, onto your bottom palm as if you are chopping something in half.

Can/could/able/ possible

With your palms facing out, make your fists into either an "A" or "S" handshape (see pages 2–3)—the location of your thumb isn't incredibly important—then drop both fists down at the wrists. Repeat this movement to sign **ABLE** or **POSSIBLE**.

Ask

Place both hands in flat handshapes with your palms facing each other. Rotate your hands up and bring your palms together until they touch. The final position of the sign looks like your hands are in prayer.

Need/must/ should/have to

Make an "X" handshape (see page 3) with one hand like a hook and pull your whole hand as if you are pulling down on a cord. This is also the sign for **MUST**, **SHOULD**, and **HAVE TO**.

Can't

With your palms facing down, make fists and then stick out both index fingers, with one hovering above the other. Bring your top finger down and knock your other finger as you pass by it. To remember the sign, think of a child reaching to touch something hot and their parent knocking their finger out of the way so they don't get burned.

Help/
Can I help you?/
Can you help me?

Hold out one hand in a flat handshape, palm facing up, in front of your body. With your other hand in an "A" handshape (see page 2), set it on the palm of your other hand. If you move this sign toward someone with a questioning look on your face, you are signing "**CAN I HELP YOU?**" If you move the sign toward you with a questioning look, you are signing, "**CAN YOU HELP ME?**"

Happy

With your palm facing in and flat on your chest, bring your hand upward repeatedly while smiling and making a happy expression on your face.

Excited/ What's up?/thrilled

With your palms facing toward your body, make a "5" handshape (see page 4) with your middle fingers bent in. Then, with a joyful expression on your face, make alternating inward circular motions with your hands, tapping your middle fingers to your chest as you go. If you change this sign so your hands move upward at the same time, it becomes the sign for **WHAT'S UP** or **THRILLED**.

Fine

With your palm facing to the side, make a 5 handshape (see page 4) and tap your thumb to your chest a few times.

Hurt/headache/ stomachache

With your palms facing in, place your hands in front of your chest and point your index fingers at each other. Then twist your hands in opposite directions from the wrist. Sign this near your head for **HEADACHE**, or near your stomach for **STOMACHACHE**.

Sad

With your palms facing in, make a "5" handshape (see page 4) on each side of your face. Pull your hands downward as if your face is drooping with sadness. Be sure to make a sad facial expression as you do this sign.

Frustrated

With your palm facing out, make a flat closed-fingered handshape in front of your chin. Bring your hand back to tap the back of your fingers against your chin a few times. Show a look of frustration as you do this sign.

Scared

Starting with your fists in front of your chest, palms facing in, quickly open your hands into the "5" handshape (see page 4) with a frightened look on your face.

Angry/grumpy

With your palm facing in, make a "5" handshape (see page 4) in front of your face and close your fingers abruptly into a claw. If you repeat this movement, it becomes the sign for **GRUMPY**.

Bored

With your palm facing out and hand in the "1" handshape, touch it against the side of your nose. Rotate your hand so your palm ends up facing you. Make a bored and uninterested look as you do this sign.

Curious

With one hand, make an "F" handshape (see page 2). Pinch a little bit of the skin on the front of your neck and wiggle your hand. Make an expression of curiosity as you do this sign.

Jealous

With your palm facing to the side, make an "X" handshape (see page 3). Touch your index finger to your cheek and then twist your palm toward you, keeping the "X" handshape while making an envious expression.

Proud

With your palm facing down, make an "A" handshape (see page 2). Touch the tip of your thumb to the bottom of your chest and pull your hand up in a straight line. Make a proud expression on your face as you do this sign.

Tired

With your palms facing toward each other in front of your shoulders, make a "5" hand- shape (see page 4), with both hands bent down at the wrist. Curl both hands down, rotating toward your body at the wrist, until your palms face away from each other, as if your body is slumping from exhaustion. Show a tired look on your face.

Embarrassed

With your palms facing in, make a "5" handshape (see page 4) on either side of your face. Move your hands alternately in an upward circular motion, as if you were flushing from embarrassment.

Surprised

With both hands in fists, pinch your thumbs and index fingers together next to your eyes. Then open the two fingers suddenly as if you saw something surprising. Show a look of surprise on your face.

Silly

With your palm facing to the side, make a "Y" handshape (see page 3). Touch your thumb to your nose and move your hand side to side with a silly or joking look on your face.

Lonely

Touch your index finger to your chin and move it in a downward circular motion a few times. Make a sad facial expression as you do this sign.

Feel/sensitive

With your palm facing in, make a "5" hand-shape (see page 4) and tilt your middle finger in until it touches your chest. Bring your hand up repeatedly, as if you were stroking your heart. If you make this sign in a downward motion, it becomes the sign for **SENSITIVE**.

Laugh/smile

Touch the sides of your mouth with your index fingers and stroke them outward repeatedly as if drawing a happy face. If you do this sign with just one movement, it is the sign for **SMILE**.

Cry

With the other fingers in a fist, touch your index fingers to your cheeks below your eyes, and move them downward repeatedly, as if tears are streaming down your cheeks. Make a sad face as you do this sign.

Sports/athletics/ competition/race

With your palms facing each other, make an "A" handshape (see page 2) with both hands. Then brush your knuckles back and forth against each other a few times. This is also the sign for **ATHLETICS**, **COMPETITION**, and **RACE**!

Soccer/kick

With your palms facing toward your body and fingers pointing sideways, make a flat handshape with your dominant hand and a loose fist with the other. Hold the hand in a loose fist and bring your other hand up to knock the bottom of that hand several times, as if you are "kicking" it. If you do this sign once, it is the sign for **KICK**.

Baseball

Hold your closed fists together, one above the other, as if you are holding a baseball bat, and make a couple of small swinging motions.

Basketball

There are several ways to sign **BASKETBALL**. The most common way is to make a "3" handshape (see page 4) on both hands, palms facing each other, and rock your hands back and forth. Imagine you are holding a basketball and getting ready to toss it!

Football

Make a "5" handshape (see page 4) on both hands, palms facing each other, and bring your hands together to interlock your fingers, almost like players tackling each other. Repeat this movement twice.

Play

With palms facing in, make a "Y" hand-shape (see page 3) with both hands. Then twist your wrists outward and inward at least two times. This is the sign for the verb **PLAY**. If you want to say, "I am going to act in a **PLAY**," you would use a different sign (see **THEATRE**, page 37).

Team/family

With your palms facing out, make a "T" handshape (see page 3) with both hands. Touch your index fingers together and then rotate them away from you until your pinkie fingers meet and your palms are facing you. To sign **FAMILY**, make this sign with "F" handshapes (see page 2).

Game

With your palms facing in, make "A" hand-shapes (see page 2) with both hands and gently bang your knuckles against each other repeatedly.

Win

Make a fist with one hand. Make your other hand into a "C" handshape (see page 2) and close it into a fist as you brush across the top of the other fist.

Lose

Hold one hand out in a flat handshape with your palm facing up. Make a "V" hand-shape (see page 3) with your other hand, and slap it across your flat palm. Note that this is the sign for when you lose a game or a match, but not the sign for when you lose an object, like a pen.

Walking

With your palms facing down, make flat or slightly bent handshapes with both hands. Alternately move your hands back and forth, like feet walking on the ground.

Bicycle/biking

Hold both hands out in front of you as if you are holding the handlebars of a bike. Then make alternating circular motions with your fists to mimic the motion of pedaling a bicycle.

Dance

Place one hand in a flat handshape in front of your body with your palm facing up. Make a "V" handshape (see page 3) with your other hand, pointing your fingertips down to the flat hand. Sweep your "V" hand back and forth along your flat hand, like legs across a dance floor.

Art/drawing

Place one hand in a flat handshape in front of your body, palm facing up. Make an "I" handshape (see page 2) with your other hand and touch your pinkie to your flat hand. Then "draw" an imaginary squiggly line down your palm, just like you're drawing with a pen on paper.

Paint

Make a flat handshape with one hand, palm facing to the side and fingers pointing up. Then make a flat handshape with your other hand, palm facing down, and brush your fingertips up and down the vertical hand, as if you're painting at an easel with a paintbrush.

Music

Make both hands into flat handshapes. Hold one hand in front of your body, palm facing up. Swing your other hand, palm facing to the side, back and forth above your bottom arm.

Photography

Make both hands into an "L" handshape (see page 2) and hold them on either side of your forehead. With your dominant hand, wiggle your index finger up and down as if you are snapping pictures on a camera.

Theatre/play/ perform/drama

With your palms facing each other, make an "A" handshape (see page 2) with both hands. Touch the tips of your thumbs against your chest and move them in alternating downward circles. This is also the sign for **PLAY** (noun), **PERFORM**, and **DRAMA**.

Movie

Make both hands into a "5" handshape (see page 4). Touch your palms together with the fingers of one hand pointing in a relaxed sideways position and the fingers of the other hand pointing up. Rock the hand with your fingers facing up against your other palm in a repeated motion.

Travel/trip

With your palm facing down, make a bent "V" handshape (see page 3), which resembles the front wheels of a car. Move the hand away from your body, as if you are moving a car forward to go on a trip. This is also the sign for **TRIP**.

Hungry

With your palm facing in, make a "C" handshape (page 2) at the top of your chest and drag it down to your stomach. If you want to show that you are very hungry, sign the word slowly.

Full

With your palm facing down, make a flat handshape in front of your chest. Then bring your hand up to hit the bottom of your chin—as if you ate so much food, it filled you up all the way to the top of your throat!

Thirsty

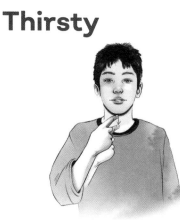

With your palm facing toward you, point your index finger up and draw a line down your throat as if you're showing that your throat is dry and you need a drink.

Food/eat

Hold your hand in front of your mouth and touch all of your fingers together as if you are holding a piece of food. Then touch your fingertips to your mouth like you're putting the food in your mouth. This is also the sign for **EAT**.

Drink

Make a "C" handshape (see page 2), like you are holding a cup. Then bring your hand up to your mouth like you're tilting the cup to take a drink.

Breakfast/lunch/dinner

With your palm facing to the side, make a "B" handshape (see page 2) and hold your hand up to your mouth. Gently tap your fingers to your mouth as you make a circular motion. Change your hand-shape to "L" to sign **LUNCH**, and to "D" to sign **DINNER**.

Fruit

With your palm facing in, make an "F" handshape (page 2). Touch your pinched thumb and index finger to your cheek and then twist them back and forth.

Vegetables

Make a "V" handshape (see page 3). Touch your index finger to your cheek and twist your hand back and forth.

Cookie

Hold out your hand in a flat handshape with your palm facing up. With your other hand, make a claw handshape and touch your fingertips to your palm, then twist your wrist and touch down on your palm again as if you are cutting cookie dough with a cookie cutter.

Cheese

Place your hands horizontally in front of you with your palms facing toward each other. Make a "5" handshape (see page 4) with each hand and then press your top palm to your bottom palm. Twist your top palm a couple of times as if you're pressing moisture out of cheese.

Pizza

With your palm facing up, bring your fingertips toward your mouth as if you're holding a slice of pizza and about to take a bite!

Hamburger

Cross one palm over the other in front of your body. Squeeze your hands together as if you're shaping a ball of hamburger meat into a patty, then switch your hands so the bottom hand ends up on top.

Hot dog

With your palms facing down, touch your fists together, end to end. Then open your fists slightly, moving your hands outward, then bunch them into fists again, as if you're squeezing the ends of a hot dog.

Spaghetti

With your palms facing in toward your body, make an "I" handshape (see page 2) with each hand, pointing your pinkies toward each other. Then move your pinkies away from each other, making little curling motions as you go.

Milk

With your palm facing to the side, make a fist. Then squeeze it open and closed as if you are milking a cow.

Cereal

Make a "1" handshape (page 4) with your palm facing down, touch the side of your chin with your index finger, and then wiggle your finger side to side across your chin.

Water

With your palm facing to the side, make a "W" handshape (see page 3) and tap the side of your chin a couple of times as if you are bringing the edge of a cup to your face.

Juice

Using your pinkie finger, draw a small letter "J" on your cheek.

Ice cream

Hold your fist up to your mouth as if you're holding an ice-cream cone and move it up and down as if you are licking it!

Candy

With your palm facing out, hold your index fingertip up to your cheek and then twist your hand back and forth. Think of the dimple of a child's smile when someone gives them candy!

Outside/leave

With your palm facing in, make a "5" hand-shape (see page 4) near the upper side of your head. Bring all of your fingertips together in a pulling motion away from you. Do this twice. If you do this sign with just one pulling motion, it becomes the sign for **LEAVE**.

Nature

Hold both hands in front of you, palms facing down. Make a "U" handshape (see page 3) with your top hand and a closed fist with your bottom hand. Make a slight circular motion with your top hand, then bring it down to land your fingertips on the top of your fist.

Tree

Hold one arm across your body with your hand out flat as if you're resting on a flat surface. Make a "5" handshape (see page 4) with your other hand and rest that elbow on top of your bottom hand. Twist your top hand at the wrist a few times like a tree shaking its branches.

Grass

With your palm facing up, make a claw handshape and touch your palm to your chin a few times in an outward motion. Think of lying on your stomach in the grass and the blades sticking up around your face.

Sun

With your palm facing to the side, make a "C" handshape (see page 2) and touch it to the side of your face. Then raise your hand away from your head, like the sun rising into the sky.

Moon

This is very similar to the sign for **SUN**. With your palm facing to the side, make a "C" handshape (see page 2) with just your index finger and thumb. Touch your thumb to the side of your face and raise your hand up and away from your head, like a crescent moon rising.

Flower

With your palm facing to the side and slightly bent, bring all of your fingertips together and touch them to one side of your nose. Then rotate the fingers around your nose to touch them to the other side, as if you are smelling flowers.

Star

With your palms facing out, point both index fingers up. Brush your index fingers against each other in an up and down movement, like you are pointing up at the stars.

Weather

With both hands facing out, make a "5" handshape (see page 4) with both hands and move them down in a squiggly motion, keeping your fingers straight.

Winter/cold

With your palms facing together, hold up both your fists in front of your chest. Shake your fists in and out as if you are shivering. To use this sign to say **COLD**, make a facial expression that shows you are freezing. If you're using this sign to say **WINTER**, then do not make a facial expression.

Spring

With your palm facing to the side, make a loose fist in front of your body. With your other hand, touch all of your fingertips together, palm facing in, and push your hand through the open fist while opening up your fingers, like a flower blooming.

Summer

With your palm facing down, point your index finger and hold it up to the opposite side of your forehead. Then pull your index finger across your forehead as you bend it into an "X" handshape (see page 3), as if you are wiping sweat off your brow.

Autumn/fall

With your palm facing down, make a "5" handshape (see page 4) and brush your hand against the elbow of your opposite arm a few times, as if you're brushing leaves off the sleeve of your jacket.

Hot

With your palm facing in, make a claw handshape and cover your mouth. Then rotate your hand outward, away from your face, as if you can't stand the heat!

Rain

With your palms facing out, make a "5" handshape (see page 4) with both hands in front of your face. Drop your hands down at the wrist a few times, like falling raindrops.

Snow

With your palms facing out, make a "5" handshape (see page 4) with both hands in front of your face. Drop your arms down a few times while wiggling your fingers, like a flurry of snowflakes.

Wind

With your palms wide apart and facing each other, make a "5" handshape (see page 4) with both hands and sway your hands from side to side.

Thunder

Point to your ear with one index finger, then make fists with both hands, palms facing down. Shake your fists side to side, like you are a loud clap of thunder shaking the ground.

Lightening

With your palm facing out in a "1" hand-shape, use your index finger to draw a jagged line downward, as if you are drawing the shape of a lightning bolt.

School

With your palms facing each other and your hands in flat handshapes, hold both hands horizontally in front of your body. Tap your top flat palm against your bottom flat palm a couple times as if you're clapping for getting a good grade!

Study

Hold out one hand in a flat handshape with your palm facing up. With your other hand, make a "5" handshape (see page 4) and point your fingertips down at your palm and wiggle your fingers.

Learn/student/person

To sign **LEARN**, hold out your hand in a flat handshape, palm facing up. Touch the fingertips of your other hand to your flat palm and pull them together in an upward movement as if you are pulling information out of a book. To turn this sign into **STUDENT**, after signing **LEARN**, immediately change both of your hands into flat handshapes side by side, palms facing together, and move them straight downward. (When signed on its own, this is the sign for **PERSON**.)

Read

With your palm facing up or to the side, hold out a flat handshape. With your other hand, make a "V" handshape (see page 3) and point your fingertips toward your flat palm. Drop your fingers down your palm, as if your fingertips are two eyes scrolling down the page of a book.

Write

With your palm facing up, hold out your hand in a flat handshape. With your other hand, hold your thumb and index finger together like you're holding a pencil and make a writing motion across your flat palm.

History

With your palm facing to the side, make an "H" handshape (see page 2). Then move your hand up and down at the wrist in a chopping motion.

English

With the palm of one hand facing down, make a loose fist with your other hand and place it on top of your flat hand. Move both hands slightly inwards, towards your body.

Math/algebra/ geometry

With your palms facing together, make the "M" handshape (see page 2) with both hands, and place one hand slightly higher than the other. Moving your hands horizontally, brush your hands against each other a couple of times. Make an "A" handshape for **ALGEBRA**, or a "G" handshape for **GEOMETRY**.

Science

With your palms facing out, make an "A" handshape (see page 2) with both hands. Then move them alternately in a circular motion.

Language

With your palms facing down and thumbs almost touching, make an "L" handshape (see page 2) with both hands. Then move your hands away from each other in a wiggling motion to your sides.

Technology

Hold up one hand in a flat handshape, horizontally, with your palm facing in. Then, with your other hand in a "5" handshape (page 4), tap the middle finger of your other hand to the bottom of your top hand a few times.

Gym

With your palms facing your body and fingers pointing up, make loose fists with both hands. Then make small circular motions with your hands and upper arms, as if you are jumping rope.

Teach/teacher

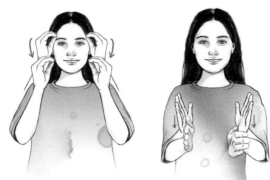

To sign **TEACH**, make a flat "O" handshape (see page 2) with both hands in front of your face, palms facing together, and move your hands out and down in a repeated movement. To sign **TEACHER**, after signing **TEACH**, change your hands to flat handshapes, palms facing together and move them straight down to sign **PERSON**.

Class

With your palms facing out, make a "C" handshape (see page 2) with both hands. Then circle your hands around in a forward motion until your palms are facing you, as if you are creating a bubble around a group of people.

Book

Hold up both hands in a flat handshape with your palms touching. Then open your palms while keeping the pinkie side of your hands touching, as if you are opening a book.

Library

With your palm facing out, make an "L" handshape (see page 2) and then move your hand in a circular motion.

Test

With your palms facing out, point your index fingers up and repeatedly bend them into "X" handshapes (see page 3) as you move your hands downward.

Homework

Close the fingertips of one hand together and bring them to your cheek as if you are going to sign **HOME** (page 14). With your other hand, make a fist out in front of you, palm facing down. Then change the handshape of your top hand into a fist and drop it down to hit your bottom fist to sign **WORK**.

Smart

With your palm facing to the side, tap your middle finger to your forehead, keeping the rest of your fingers straight. Then twist your hand until your palm is facing out.

Deaf

With your palm facing to the side, touch your index finger near your mouth, then bring your finger up to touch near your ear.

Hearing

With your hand in a "1" handshape (see page 4) and palm facing down, touch your index finger just below your lip and make forward circular motions, like sounds coming out of your mouth.

Good

Hold out one hand in a flat handshape with your palm facing up. Touch the fingertips of your other flat hand to your mouth or chin, then bring that hand down to meet your other hand with both palms facing up.

Bad

Hold out one hand in a flat handshape with your palm facing up. Touch the fingertips of your other flat hand to your mouth or chin, then bring the hand down toward your bottom hand as if you are about to sign **GOOD**, but quickly flip your palm so it slaps onto your bottom palm to sign **BAD**.

Purple

With your palm facing in, hold up a "P" handshape (see page 3) in front of your chest and rotate your wrist so your palm turns out and back a couple of times.

Green

With your palm facing to the side, make a "G" handshape (see page 2) and twist your wrist so your palm turns out and in a few times.

Red

Touch the tip of your index finger to your chin and pull your finger downward into an "X" handshape (see page 3).

Blue

With your palm facing in, hold up a "B" handshape (see page 2) and twist your wrist so your palm turns in and out a few times.

Black

With your palm facing down, point your index finger to the opposite side of your forehead and drag the side of your finger across your forehead in a line.

Brown/tan

With your palm facing out, make a "B" handshape (page 2) and touch your index finger to your cheek. Slide your hand down the side of your face in a straight line. If you do this sign with a "T" handshape, it becomes the sign for **TAN**.

White

With your palm facing in, start by holding a "5" handshape (see page 4) to your chest. Then close all of your fingertips together as you pull the hand away from your chest.

Yellow

With your palm facing in, make a "Y" handshape (see page 3) in front of you and twist your wrist so your palm turns out and in a few times.

Orange

With your palm facing to the side, hold a fist up to your chin and open and close your fingers in a squeezing motion, just like you are squeezing juice from an orange.

Pink

With your palm facing in, make a "P" handshape (see page 3) and draw a small line down your chin with your middle finger. This movement can either be done once or twice.

Small

Make flat handshapes with both palms facing each other and move your hands in and out repeatedly without touching, as if you are showing the size of a small animal. When doing this sign, squeeze your lips into a tiny "o" shape, like you are saying "oooh."

Medium

Make both hands into flat handshapes with one slightly above the other. Face the top palm to the side and the bottom palm toward your body, pinkie-side down. With your top hand, make a small chopping motion into the middle part of your bottom hand. When you make this sign, purse your lips together tightly.

Big/large

Hold your hands in front of your body, palms facing each other, and make an "L" handshape (see page 2) with both hands and your index fingers bent. Pull your hands away from each other as if you're showing something growing bigger. When you make this sign, move your mouth to look like you are saying "cha."

Square/circle/triangle/rectangle

Point both your index fingers forward and use them both to draw a square in the air in front of you. You also use your index fingers this way to draw other shapes like **CIRCLE**, **TRIANGLE**, and **RECTANGLE**.

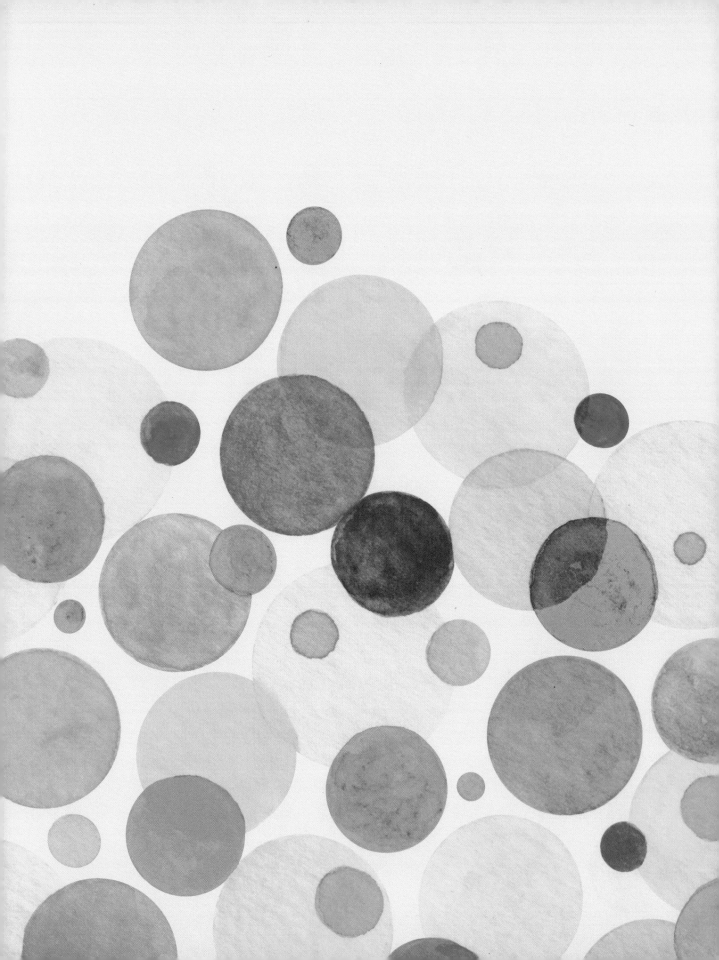

PART 2

Sign Language Activities

🖐 Fingerspelling Practice

Now that you have learned to sign the alphabet, let's practice putting letters together to make words! Remember to focus on forming the letters properly, rather than speed.

Fun	Zoo	Yes	Am
Pool	Hop	Make	Box
We	Pig	Or	Shoe
Cat	Itch	Pop	Door
Dog	Let	Bike	Fan
Mom	Go	See	Cup
Big	Jump	Top	
Feel	No	Van	

🧩 Grammar Practice

Practice signing each of the English sentences below using correct ASL grammar. Remember, ASL is a topic-comment language. Also remember that questions are expressed at the end of the sentence. Many small English words are not needed in ASL, such as *it, is, am, be, are,* and *to.* Answers on page 108.

1. **I need to go to the bathroom.**

2. **Do you want to practice ASL?**

3. **Are you excited for school?**

4. **I feel tired.**

5. **Do you like dancing?**

6. **Do you have a good book?**

Matching

Let's find out how many signs you remember! Draw a line from each sign below to its matching English word. Afterward, practice the signs that you forgot. Answers on page 108.

Understand

Book

Know

Brother

Hungry

Ask

Maybe

Hello

🔍 Signing Sleuth!

I am thinking of five signs that we have learned together. I have given you some clues to help you figure out which signs I am thinking of. Let's see if you can figure out these five mystery words! Answers on page 108.

1. I am thinking of something sweet that is baked in an oven. It can be crunchy or soft, and is usually round, but can be other shapes too.

2. I am thinking of something in nature. It is usually green, but can also be brown. It grows fast and needs to be cut often.

3. I am thinking of something that can be found in a school, but also outside of school. People go there to get strong and usually leave sweaty.

4. I am thinking of something you can see in the night sky. It looks small but is really very large and sometimes looks like it is twinkling.

5. I am thinking of a feeling that makes you want to lay down. You usually close your eyes when you feel this way.

 Sign a Song!

Do you have a favorite song that you would like to sign? It would be best to pick one that is simple and uses a lot of the signs you have learned so far. If you would like, you can even make up a new song!

There will be some words that you do not know the signs for yet and that is okay. You can either just spell the words you do not know, or look them up in an ASL dictionary. If you have a friend or family member who knows ASL, ask them if they would be willing to teach you some of the new signs. As you practice, you will become more fluent and be able to sign more quickly and clearly.

A couple of my favorite simple songs to practice with are:

If You're Happy and You Know It

Happy Birthday to You

The Alphabet Song

Twinkle, Twinkle, Little Star

Another fun way to practice signing songs is by listening to the radio and signing along as much as you can.

Secret Message

This crossword puzzle is solved a bit differently from what you might be used to. It has a secret message inside it! Each ASL letter below has a number before it. Identify the ASL letter, then find the box with the number in the crossword and write the letter in the box. When all the boxes are filled in, descramble the words to figure out the secret message! Answers on page 108.

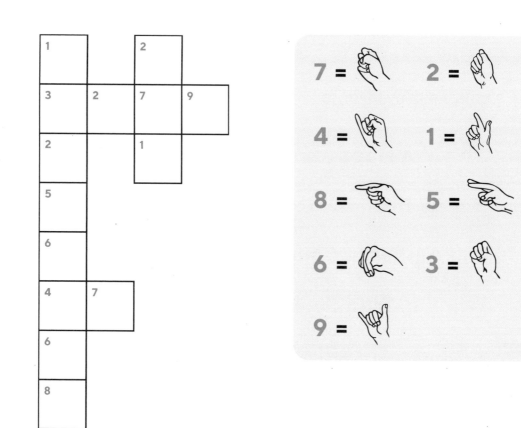

SECRET MESSAGE:

__ __ __ __ __ __

__ __ __   __ __   __ __ __ __ .

? Guess the Food

Let's find out which signs you remember the best! Below, I've given you 10 signs that have to do with food. Can you guess what each sign is? After you are done, check the answer key to see how many you identified correctly. Answers on page 108.

1. _____

2. _____

3. _____

4. _____

5. _____

6. _____

7. _____

8. _____

9. _____

10. _____

What Did I Say?

Here, I have signed eight sentences in ASL. Sign along with me and see if you can figure out what I am saying. Refer to the grammar rules in the introduction (page vii) as needed to remember how ASL and English sentence structures are different. Answers on page 108.

Word Search

Have you ever done a word search before? Are you good at spotting words in a jumble of letters? How about words in a jumble of hands? I have mixed eight fingerspelled words among a bunch of signed letters. The words can be vertical, horizontal, or diagonal. Let's see how many you can find! Answers on page 109.

computer	grandma	from	hello
maybe	uncle	kitchen	brother

⭐ Lights, Camera, Sign!

Since ASL is a visual language, it is important for you to become comfortable communicating with your face and body. A good way to practice this is by acting things out. Think of old silent movies. The actors did not use words or sounds, but they were able to tell a story using only body language.

For this activity, start by picking a scene from a movie. Imagine that you are in the scene and try to act it out without using any words or sounds. If you have a friend or family member that would like to do this activity with you, choose a character for each of you. Then act out the scene together. Don't forget to use your facial expressions to show how your character is feeling.

Here are some of my favorite movies to choose scenes from:

The Lion King

Despicable Me

Harry Potter

Charlotte's Web

Shark Tale

The Incredibles

Shrek

Fingerspelling Practice

Now that you are becoming more comfortable with signing, let's practice some more fingerspelled words! Remember to focus on clarity rather than speed.

Home	Dress	Right	Card
Sore	Prize	Save	Print
Able	Yell	Talk	Book
Light	Over	Jump	Swing
Make	Next	Stuck	Pen
Less	Paper	Wing	Write
Baby	Quiet	Bowl	
Cake	Need	Goat	

Grammar Practice

Practice signing each of the English sentences below using correct ASL grammar. Remember, ASL is a topic-comment language. Also remember that questions are expressed at the end of the sentence. Also, many small English words are not needed in ASL, such as *it, is, am, be, are,* and *to.* Answers on page 109.

1. I don't like hot dogs.

2. Where is your mom?

3. Is your dog nice?

4. Do you understand the teacher?

5. I'm studying for the test.

6. I like fruits and vegetables.

Matching

Let's find out how many signs you remember! Draw a line from each sign below to its matching English word. Afterward, practice the signs that you forgot. Answers on page 109.

Grass

Food

Hurt

Excuse me

Want

Bathroom

School

Play

🔍 Signing Sleuth!

I am thinking of five signs that we have learned together. I have given you some clues to help you figure out which signs I am thinking of. Let's see if you can figure out these five mystery words! Answers on page 109.

1. **I am thinking of something that is round and very hot. It is out only in the daytime. We need it to help things grow.**

   _____

2. **I am thinking of something that helps us communicate when we are apart. You can carry it with you in a purse or pocket.**

   _____

3. **I am thinking of something that is a rectangle shape. It is in most houses. People like to watch it.**

   _____

4. **I am thinking of something people do when they see or read something funny. It is usually done while smiling.**

   _____

5. **I am thinking of a place where people go to read or re-search. It is very quiet and has lots and lots of shelves.**

   _____

⭐ Tell Me a Story

Storytelling is an important part of Deaf culture and something that is very cherished by the Deaf community. For this activity, start by picking out a children's book or fairytale. Go through the story and find all the words that you know the signs for. If you have a friend or family member who knows ASL, ask them if they will help you learn more signs to words that are in your story.

Practice telling the story using signs, body language, and facial expressions. Once you have practiced a few times and feel confident, find an audience to tell your story to. This can be your mom, dad, grandparents, siblings, or friends. Two of my favorite stories to sign are *Goldilocks and the Three Bears* and *The Three Little Pigs*. You can include a lot of gestures and body language in both of these stories.

Secret Message

This crossword puzzle is solved a bit differently from what you might be used to. It has a secret message inside it! Each ASL letter below has a number before it. Identify the ASL letter, then find the box with the number in the crossword and write the letter in the box. When all the boxes are filled in, descramble the words to figure out the secret message! Answers on page 109.

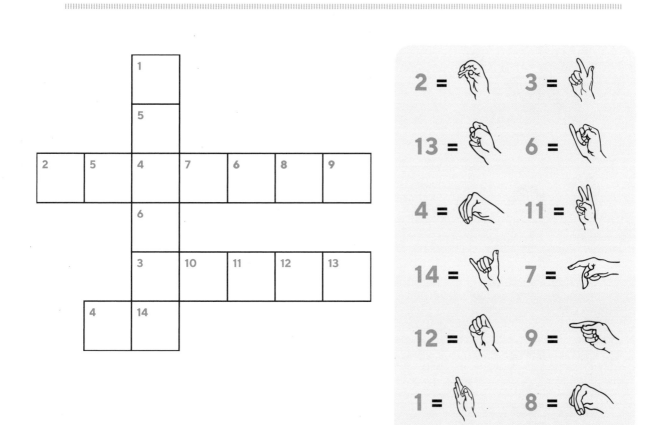

SECRET MESSAGE:

___ ___   ___ ___ ___ ___ ___   ___ ___ ___

___ ___ ___ ___ ___ ___ ___.

? Guess the Activity

Let's find out which signs you remember the best! Below, I've given you 10 signs that represent activities. Can you guess what each sign is? After you are done, check the answer key to see how many you identified correctly. Answers on page 109.

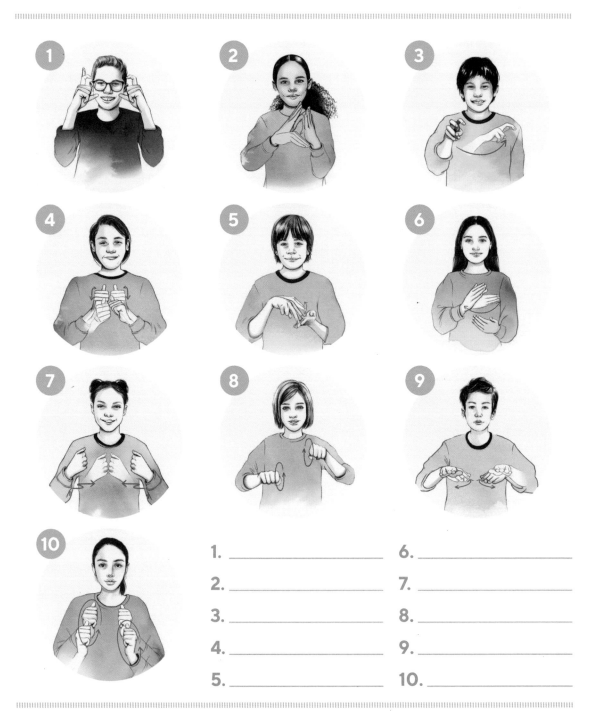

1. _____   6. _____

2. _____   7. _____

3. _____   8. _____

4. _____   9. _____

5. _____   10. _____

What Did I Say?

Here, I have signed eight sentences in ASL. Sign along with me and see if you can figure out what I am saying. Refer to the grammar rules in the introduction (page vii) as needed to remember how ASL and English sentence structures are different. Answers on page 109.

Word Search

Have you ever done a word search before? Are you good at spotting words in a jumble of letters? How about words in a jumble of hands? I have mixed eight fingerspelled words among a bunch of signed letters. The words can be vertical, horizontal, or diagonal. Let's see how many you can find! Answers on page 109.

| daughter | phone | here | name |
| bedroom | please | why | baby |

 Charades

Find a dictionary and choose someone to go first. That person picks a word from the dictionary and acts it out for everyone else. Remember not to use any spoken words or sounds! Set a timer for one minute. If someone guesses the word before the timer goes off, the "actor" gets a point. Then it's the next person's turn. Play until someone has five points. The winner then gets to choose a super long English word for the other players to fingerspell.

Here are some long words that would be fun to try.

Encyclopedia

Birthday

Snoring

Locomotive

Snorkeling

Fingerspelling

Now that you are becoming more comfortable with signing, let's practice some more fingerspelled words! Remember to focus on clarity rather than speed.

Sticky	Juice	Country	Kitten
Printer	Pizza	Pencil	Summer
Note	Letter	Blanket	River
Staple	Lucky	Rainbow	Magic
Bath	School	Lizard	Garbage
Lamp	Clouds	Jumping	Parking
Grass	Street	Sweatshirt	
Treetop	Ocean	Floor	

Grammar Practice

Practice signing each of the English sentences below using correct ASL grammar. Remember, ASL is a topic-comment language. Also remember that questions are expressed at the end of the sentence. Also, many small English words are not needed in ASL, such as *it, is, am, be, are,* and *to.* Answers on page 109.

1. **What is your brother's name?**

2. **My cat is orange and white.**

3. **I am going to science class.**

4. **The kitchen is big.**

5. **Will you help me practice?**

6. **Do you play baseball?**

☀ Matching

Let's find out how many signs you remember! Draw a line from each sign below to its matching English word. Afterward, practice the signs that you forgot. Answers on page 109.

Pizza

Math

Practice

Mom

Sorry

Basketball

Bored

Read

🔍 Signing Sleuth!

I am thinking of five signs that we have learned together. I have given you some clues to help you figure out which signs I am thinking of. Let's see if you can figure out these five mystery words! Answers on page 109.

1. I am thinking of something people like to do when they hear music. They use their bodies and can move quickly or slowly.

2. I am thinking of something people drink that is usually white. It comes from an animal and is usually served cold.

3. I am thinking of something that is very loud and usually happens right after a big flash of light. Some people get scared when they hear it.

4. I am thinking of something people usually do in warmer weather. It involves moving your legs to turn wheels.

5. I am thinking of a topic you study in school. It about events and people from the past.

⭐ Read My Lips

Have you ever wondered how Deaf/hard-of-hearing (hh) people read lips? Do you think it is easy or difficult? Only 30–45% of what we say can actually be understood through lip reading. Things like facial hair that covers part of the mouth, enunciation, speed, and other variables all effect a person's ability to read a person's lips.

   For this activity, find a friend or family member and take turns saying words to each other without making any actual sounds. To make this more challenging, try saying complete phrases or sentences.

Here are some words and phrases to get you started:

Brush your teeth.

I love you!

Do you need to go to the bathroom?

Where is my backpack?

Let's go on a road trip!

Secret Message

This crossword puzzle is solved a bit differently from what you might be used to. It has a secret message inside it! Each ASL letter below has a number before it. Identify the ASL letter, then find the box with the number in the crossword and write the letter in the box. When all the boxes are filled in, descramble the words to figure out the secret message! Answers on page 109.

9 =

8 =

5 =

12 =

2 =

1 =

6 =

7 =

3 =

4 =

13 =

10 =

11 =

SECRET MESSAGE:

___ ___ ___   ___ ___ ___ ___   ___ ___ ___ ___

___ ___ ___ ___ ___ ___ ___ .

Guess the Feeling

Let's find out which signs you remember the best! Below, I've given you 10 signs that represent feelings. Can you guess what each sign is? After you are done, check the answer key to see how many you identified correctly. Answers on page 110.

1. _____

2. _____

3. _____

4. _____

5. _____

6. _____

7. _____

8. _____

9. _____

10. _____

What Did I Say?

Here, I have signed eight sentences in ASL. Sign along with me and see if you can figure out what I am saying. Refer to the grammar rules in the introduction (page vii) as needed to remember how ASL and English sentence structures are different. Answers on page 110.

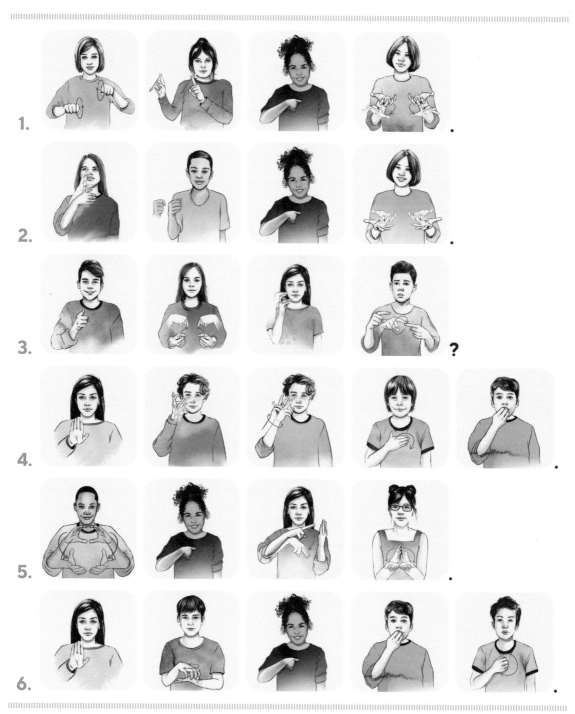

 Word Search

Have you ever done a word search before? Are you good at spotting words in a jumble of letters? How about words in a jumble of hands? I have mixed eight fingerspelled words among a bunch of signed letters. The words can be vertical, horizontal, or diagonal. Let's see how many you can find! Answers on page 110.

understand	**think**	**tell**	**need**
stop	**guess**	**practice**	**run**

 Traffic Signs

Next time you are riding in a vehicle to go somewhere, look out the window to find words that are visible all around us. Look for street signs, store fronts, billboards, license plates, and types of cars. Try fingerspelling as many of these as you can. The more you practice, the more fluent your fingerspelling will become—and the more fun your car rides will be!

🖐 Fingerspelling Practice

Now that you are becoming more comfortable with signing, let's practice some more fingerspelled words! Remember to focus on clarity rather than speed.

Pillow	Orange	Jumping jacks	Airplane
Shower	Quarter	Birthday	Vacation
Homework	Cell phone	Swimming pool	Business
Backpack	Mountain	Outside	Science
New York	School bus	Shopping	Yesterday
Sidewalk	Internet	Jellyfish	Green beans
Mailbox	Pictures	Popcorn	Applesauce
Lightning	Honeycomb		

⚙ Grammar Practice

Practice signing each of the English sentences below using correct ASL grammar. Remember, ASL is a topic–comment language. Also remember that questions are expressed at the end of the sentence. Also, many small English words are not needed in ASL, such as *it, is, am, be, are,* and *to.* Answers on page 110.

1. **Please stop laughing.**

2. **The weather outside is cold.**

3. **My bedroom is hot.**

4. **My grandpa and grandma are silly.**

5. **Do you have ice cream?**

6. **Did you win your game?**

Matching

Let's find out how many signs you remember! Draw a line from each sign below to its matching English word. Afterward, practice the signs that you forgot. Answers on page 110.

Feel

Proud

Hot

Where

Dance

Pet

Small

Cousin

🔍 Signing Sleuth!

I am thinking of five signs that we have learned together. I have given you some clues to help you figure out which signs I am thinking of. Let's see if you can figure out these five mystery words! Answers on page 110.

1. **I am thinking of a bright, cheery color. It often makes people think of sunshine. You can combine it with another color to make orange.**

   _____

2. **I am thinking of a sport. The ball used to play this sport is not round and it is both kicked and thrown.**

   _____

3. **I am thinking of a dessert food that is very cold. It comes in many different flavors and can be eaten with a spoon or licked from a stick.**

   _____

4. **I am thinking of an animal that comes in many colors. It can live both indoors and outdoors and is often good at catching mice.**

   _____

5. **I am thinking of something our teachers give us at school to measure what we have learned. It is usually best to study for one of these.**

   _____

⭐ Can I Take Your Order?

Imagine that you are a server in a restaurant and you have been assigned to serve a Deaf person. Imagine how grateful they will be that you are able to communicate at least part of what you are saying in ASL! Think of some of the questions they might ask you and what your responses might be. If there are words you do not know the signs for, think of ways that you can express them through gestures or body language.

This game is fun to play with a friend, sibling, or parent. One of you can be the server and the other can be the Deaf person that has come into the restaurant. Take turns being the server and the customer.

What are some other ways that you can communicate with Deaf/hh people other than spoken language?

Secret Message

This crossword puzzle is solved a bit differently from what you might be used to. It has a secret message inside it! Each ASL letter below has a number before it. Identify the ASL letter, then find the box with the number in the crossword and write the letter in the box. When all the boxes are filled in, descramble the words to figure out the secret message! Answers on page 110.

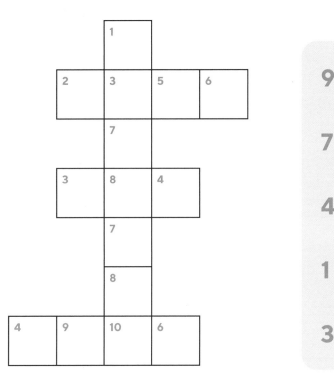

SECRET MESSAGE:

___ ___ ___ ___ ___ ___

___ ___ ___ ___   ___ ___ ___   ___ ___ ___ ___ .

❓ Guess the Weather

Let's find out which signs you remember the best! Below, I've given you 10 signs that represent seasons and weather. Can you guess what each sign is? After you are done, check the answer key to see how many you identified correctly. Answers on page 110.

1. _____

2. _____

3. _____

4. _____

5. _____

6. _____

7. _____

8. _____

9. _____

10. _____

What Did I Say?

Here, I have signed eight sentences in ASL. Sign along with me and see if you can figure out what I am saying. Refer to the grammar rules in the introduction (page vii) as needed to remember how ASL and English sentence structures are different. Answers on page 110.

◉ Word Search

Have you ever done a word search before? Are you good at spotting words in a jumble of letters? How about words in a jumble of hands? I have mixed eight fingerspelled words among a bunch of signed letters. The words can be vertical, horizontal, or diagonal. Let's see how many you can find! Answers on page 110.

| misunderstand | have | want | square | black |
| help | come | joy | pink |

⭐ Hotel Desk Clerk

You will need at least one other person for this game. For the first round, have one player be a hotel desk clerk and the other be a Deaf hotel customer. The player who is pretending to be the Deaf customer thinks of something that might be wrong with his/her hotel room.

Here are some ideas:

Room is too cold

Bugs in the bathtub

No volume on the TV

Stinky blankets

Overflowing toilet

The Deaf customer acts out what his/her issue is while the other person guesses. For the next round, switch roles and pick a different problem. See how many different issues you can come up with. Remember to take turns being the clerk and the customer. Here are some other scenarios you can try:

Grocery store clerk

Amusement park ride operator

Zookeeper

✋ Fingerspelling Practice

By now you are probably getting pretty good at fingerspelling! Let's try some really challenging words. Remember to focus on clarity rather than speed.

Soda pop	Bumblebee	Zipper	Milkshake
Everywhere	Accident	Swing set	Hand soap
Backyard	Doorbell	Avocado	Basketball
Computer	Elephant	String cheese	Tennis court
Tomorrow	Gummy bear	Notebook	Understand
Octopus	Iguana	Pine tree	Washing machine
Jump rope	Flashlight	Campfire	
Sleeping bag	Umbrella	Extra credit	

🧩 Grammar Practice

Practice signing each of the English sentences below using correct ASL grammar. Remember, ASL is a topic-comment language. Also remember that questions are expressed at the end of the sentence. Also, many small English words are not needed in ASL, such as *it, is, am, be, are,* and *to*. Answers on page 110.

1. **Do you want a cookie?**

2. **Are you excited for snow?**

3. **Why are you crying?**

4. **I will help you with your homework.**

5. **I want to write a book.**

6. **I like to travel.**

Matching

Let's find out how many signs you remember! Draw a line from each sign below to its matching English word. Afterward, practice the signs that you forgot. Answers on page 110.

Movie

Thank you

Red

Lightning

Stop

Smart

Help

Candy

🔍 Signing Sleuth!

I am thinking of five signs that we have learned together. I have given you some clues to help you figure out which signs I am thinking of. Let's see if you can figure out these five mystery words! Answers on page 111.

1. **I am thinking of something people do to see new places and experience new things. A person may take an airplane, boat, or train to do this.**

2. **I am thinking of something you might see in the wintertime when it is very cold. People can make things out of it and it makes the roads slippery.**

3. **I am thinking of the room in a house where people go to rest. It is most often used at night.**

4. **I am thinking of a food that is usually eaten at breakfast. It can be hot or cold, crunchy or soft, wet or dry, and is usually served in a bowl.**

5. **I am thinking of something people like to listen to. It uses your sense of hearing but can also be experienced through vibrations.**

⭐ Alphabet Soup

This is a game you can play alone or with friends. Start with the letter A. Choose an A word that you know the sign for. Fingerspell the word, then make the sign for it. Move on to the letter B and repeat the steps. How far into the alphabet can you go? If you come to a letter that you don't know any signs for, try to think of a word that contains that letter and use that.

   If you are playing this game with more than one person, take turns with each letter. Want an even greater challenge? Use a timer and allow ten, eight, or five seconds for each letter and see how far you can get. Reduce the time after each full alphabet round. Play until one of you can't think of a word, then start again.

Secret Message

This crossword puzzle is solved a bit differently from what you might be used to. It has a secret message inside it! Each ASL letter below has a number before it. Identify the ASL letter, then find the box with the number in the crossword and write the letter in the box. When all the boxes are filled in, descramble the words to figure out the secret message! Answers on page 111.

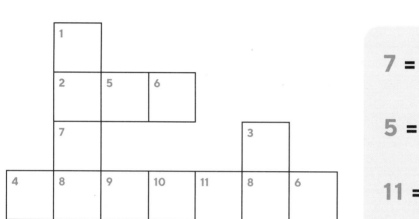

SECRET MESSAGE:

___ ___   ___ ___ ___ ___   ___ ___ ___

___ ___ ___ ___ ___ ___ ___ .

❓ Guess the Adjective

Let's find out which signs you remember the best! Below, I've given you 10 signs that represent adjectives. Can you guess what each sign is? After you are done, check the answer key to see how many you identified correctly. Answers on page 111.

1. _____   6. _____

2. _____   7. _____

3. _____   8. _____

4. _____   9. _____

5. _____   10. _____

What Did I Say?

Here, I have signed eight sentences in ASL. Sign along with me and see if you can figure out what I am saying. Refer to the grammar rules in the introduction (page vii) as needed to remember how ASL and English sentence structures are different. Answers on page 111.

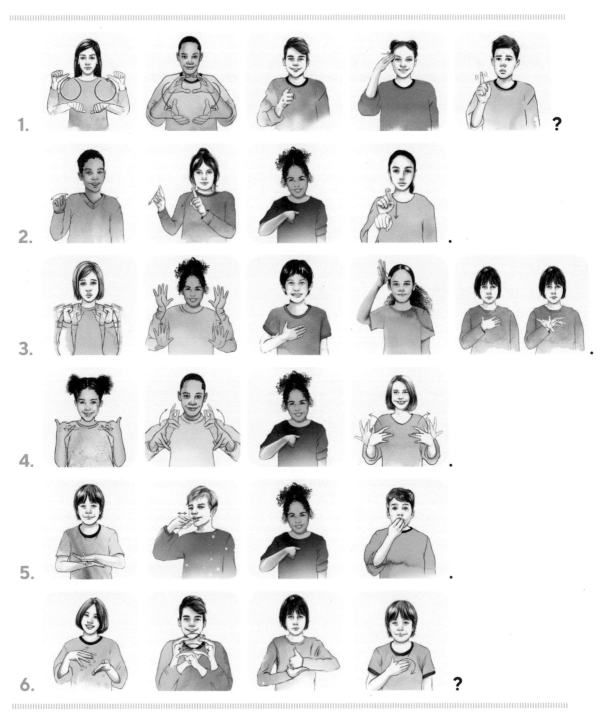

# Word Search

Have you ever done a word search before? Are you good at spotting words in a jumble of letters? How about words in a jumble of hands? I have mixed eight fingerspelled words among a bunch of signed letters. The words can be vertical, horizontal, or diagonal. Let's see how many you can find! Answers on page 111.

student	teacher	history	science	food
technology	english	school	write	

🔍 Scavenger Hunt

Let's hunt for words to sign! Choose a spot in your house to start. Set a timer for five minutes. When the timer starts, quickly look around the house for objects that you know the signs for. Sign each quickly then write it down on a piece of paper. How many words could you get in five minutes?

If you are playing with another person, compare lists at the end of the five minutes to see what different words you each discovered. Then take turns signing your word lists to each other.

ANSWER KEY

Grammar Practice, pg 62

1. Bathroom go I need.
2. Practicing ASL you want?
3. School you excited?
4. Tired me/I feel.
5. Dancing you like?
6. Good book you have?

Matching, pg 63

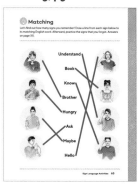

Signing Sleuth!, pg 64

Secret Message, pg 66

Guess the Food, pg 67

What Did I Say?, pg 68

1. I like spaghetti.
2. Do you want to play outside?
3. I am scared of thunder and lightning.
4. Do you like music?
5. Are you deaf or hearing?
6. Are you full?

Word Search, pg 69

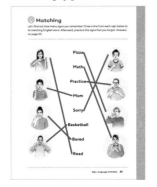

Grammar Practice, pg 71

1. Hot dogs I don't like.
2. Your mom where?
3. Your dog nice?
4. Teacher you understand?
5. Test I/me study.
6. Fruit (and) vegetables me like.

Matching, pg 72

Signing Sleuth!, pg 73

Secret Message, pg 75

Guess the Activity, pg 76

What Did I Say?, pg 77

1. Where are your brother and sister?
2. What pet do you have?
3. I'm/I going on a nature walk.
4. I don't like eating fish.
5. Can I eat breakfast outside?
6. When do you go to the library?

Word Search, pg 78

Grammar Practice, pg 80

1. Your brother name what?
2. My cat orange (and) white.
3. Science class me/I go.
4. Kitchen big.
5. Practice you help (me)?
6. Baseball you play?

Matching, pg 81

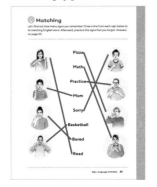

Signing Sleuth!, pg 82

Secret Message, pg 84

Guess the Feeling, pg 85

What Did I Say?, pg 86

1. I don't want to go biking.
2. I want a drink of milk.
3. When are you coming home?
4. Please eat your fruit and vegetables.
5. I am reading a book in class.
6. Sorry I ate your cookie.

Word Search, pg 87

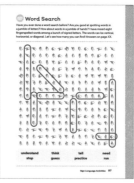

Grammar Practice, pg 89

1. Laughing please stop.
2. Outside weather cold.
3. My bedroom hot.
4. My grandma (and) grandpa silly.
5. Ice cream you have?
6. Your game win?

Matching, pg 90

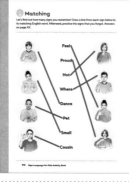

Signing Sleuth!, pg 91

1. Yellow
2. Football
3. Ice Cream
4. Cat
5. Test

Secret Message, pg 93

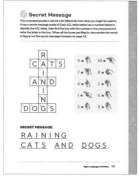

Guess the Weather, pg 94

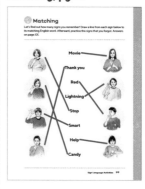

What Did I Say?, pg 95

1. Do you understand your homework?
2. My team won the soccer game.
3. My phone is in the bedroom.
4. My cat is curious.
5. Where is the purple book?
6. I want to play in the snow.

Word Search, pg 96

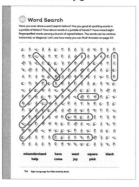

Grammar Practice, pg 98

1. Cookie you want?
2. Snow you excited?
3. You cry why?
4. Your homework I help.
5. Write book me/I want.
6. Travel I like.

Matching, pg 99

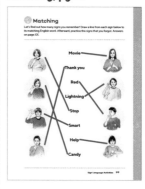

Signing Sleuth!, pg 100

Secret Message, pg 102

Guess the Adjective, pg 103

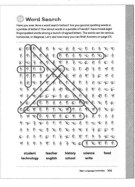

What Did I Say?, pg 104

1. Do you know where science class is?
2. I need to go to the bathroom.
3. My grandpa doesn't like cold weather.
4. I am excited to play basketball.
5. I am eating cheese pizza.
6. Help me study math, please?

Word Search, pg 105

RESOURCES

aslexpressions.com

asl-kids.com

handspeak.com/kid/

lifeprint.com

nad.org

signingtime.com

signingwithautism.com

wecansign.com

The Gallaudet Children's Dictionary of American Sign Language

ACKNOWLEDGMENTS

Thank you to my parents for never letting me use my hearing loss as an excuse, for pushing me to break through barriers, and to always advocate for myself. Mom, when the doctor told you that I probably wouldn't graduate from high school, thank you for drying your tears, stubbornly disagreeing, and making it your personal mission to prove him wrong. To my father, thank you for challenging me to reach out to others, in spite of perceived communication barriers. You inspire me to build meaningful relationships and always see the good in others. You are right, Daddy, it IS a beautiful day in the neighborhood.

Thank you, Jason, and my five kids: Ashlie, Kerrie, Ellie, Braunsen, and Rex for being my adventure buddies and for putting up with my dreadful singing voice, disappointing culinary skills, and never-ending requests to stop everything and watch a sunset. Thank you for being my number one fans, and sometimes having more faith in me than I have in myself.

Thank you, Jill Muir, the outreach consultant who encouraged my parents to introduce me to the world of signing and the Deaf community. You altered the course of my life and I will be forever grateful.

I would like to thank the teachers, administration, staff, and students at ISDB for creating a "Hogwarts world." Being there made me feel "normal" and taught me to not be ashamed of the magic of being Deaf.

Thanks also to my best friend, Emma, who has stuck around longer than anyone else, through good times and bad. Thank you for all the adventures we've had and the stories we will someday tell our grandkids (or not).

Thanks to my students, many of whom have become my closest friends and steadfast supporters. To Doris, Lana and Jeff, Angela, the O'Donnell family,

Becky, Ruth and Frances, Dave, Deseret, and so many more: you have left an imprint on my heart. I wouldn't be who I am today without you.

I would like to thank the entire team at Callisto Media for putting their faith in me. I would especially like to thank Barbara Isenberg, the editor of this project, for her enthusiasm, encouragement, and incredible eye for detail. Her own personal background in the Deaf community and extensive knowledge of ASL and Deaf culture made her an invaluable co-creator of this project. I would also like to thank the illustrator, Natalia Sanabria, for creating the most beautiful illustrations I have ever seen in an ASL book.

Lastly, I want to thank anyone who is learning sign language so you can connect with someone who cannot hear or has difficulty communicating verbally. You are giving them an incredible gift.

ABOUT THE AUTHOR

TARA ADAMS began losing her hearing as a toddler. At age 6, she was diagnosed with progressive hearing loss and by the time she was in middle school, her hearing loss was profound. Enrolling in the Idaho School for the Deaf and Blind changed her life: there, she found a community of kids just like her. Encouraged by their acceptance, she immediately pulled back her long hair, which previously had covered her hearing aids, into a ponytail. A passionate teacher was born.

Tara is the founder of ASL Expressions. She is an outspoken advocate of sign language not only for the Deaf, but also for individuals who struggle to communicate via spoken language. Tara recently founded SigningWithAutism.com and WeCanSign.com, both with the aim to spread awareness of sign language as a communication tool for non-verbal or speech-delayed children.